Know Your Numbers

SPORTS

Alex Kuskowski

Consulting Editor, Diane Craig, M.A./Reading Specialist

Sandcastle

An Imprint of Abdo Publishing
www.abdopublishing.com

visit us at www.abdopublishing.com

Published by Abdo Publishing, a division of ABDO, PO Box 398166, Minneapolis, Minnesota 55439. Copyright © 2015 by Abdo Consulting Group, Inc. International copyrights reserved in all countries. No part of this book may be reproduced in any form without written permission from the publisher. SandCastle™ is a trademark and logo of Abdo Publishing.

Printed in the United States of America, North Mankato, Minnesota
062014
092014

THIS BOOK CONTAINS
RECYCLED MATERIALS

Editor: Liz Salzmann
Content Developer: Nancy Tuminelly
Cover and Interior Design: Anders Hanson, Mighty Media, Inc.
Photo Credits: Shutterstock

Library of Congress Cataloging-in-Publication Data
Kuskowski, Alex., author.
  Know your numbers. Sports / Alex Kuskowski.
    pages cm. -- (Numbers 1-20)
  Audience: Ages 3-9.
  ISBN 978-1-62403-268-4
  1. Counting--Juvenile literature. 2. Cardinal numbers--Juvenile literature. 3. Sports--Juvenile literature. I. Title. II. Title: Sports.
  QA113.K87 2015
  513.2--dc23
                  2013041911

SandCastle™ Level: Beginning

SandCastle™ books are created by a team of professional educators, reading specialists, and content developers around five essential components—phonemic awareness, phonics, vocabulary, text comprehension, and fluency—to assist young readers as they develop reading skills and strategies and increase their general knowledge. All books are written, reviewed, and leveled for guided reading, early reading intervention, and Accelerated Reader® programs for use in shared, guided, and independent reading and writing activities to support a balanced approach to literacy instruction. The SandCastle™ series has four levels that correspond to early literacy development. The levels are provided to help teachers and parents select appropriate books for young readers.

EMERGING · **BEGINNING** · TRANSITIONAL · FLUENT

Contents

John has 1 football.
He throws it to a friend.

• = 1 = one

1 2 3 4 5 6 7 8 9 10 11 12 13 14 15 16 17 18 19 20

Erin is **skiing**. She has 2 poles to help her stand up.

1 **2** 3 4 5 6 7 8 9 10 11 12 13 14 15 16 17 18 19 20

5

Isaac plays on a basketball team.
There are 3 boys on his team.

●●● = 3 = three

1 2 **3** 4 5 6 7 8 9 10 11 12 13 14 15 16 17 18 19 20

There are 4 soccer balls.
They are different colors.

•••• = 4 = four

1 2 3 **4** 5 6 7 8 9 10 11 12 13 14 15 16 17 18 19 20

Emily plays on a kickball team.
There are 5 girls on Emily's team.

●●●●● = 5 = five

1 2 3 4 **5** 6 7 8 9 10 11 12 13 14 15 16 17 18 19 20

There are **6 croquet** balls on the field. They have white stripes.

●●●●●● = 6 = six

1 2 3 4 5 6 7 8 9 10 11 12 13 14 15 16 17 18 19 20

The track has 7 lanes. During a race, each person has a lane.

= 7 = seven

1 2 3 4 5 6 **7** 8 9 10 11 12 13 14 15 16 17 18 19 20

Rowers use oars to move the boat.
There are 8 oars.

There are 9 bikes.
They are parked in a row.

⠿ = 9 = nine

1 2 3 4 5 6 7 8 **9** 10 11 12 13 14 15 16 17 18 19 20

There are 10 baseball bats. The baseball team uses them at practice.

●●●●●
●●●●● = 10 = ten

1 2 3 4 5 6 7 8 9 **10** 11 12 13 14 15 16 17 18 19 20

Sam exercises in dance class.
There are **11** students in her class.

= **11** = eleven

1 2 3 4 5 6 7 8 9 10 **11** 12 13 14 15 16 17 18 19 20

Kayaks are boats.
There are 12 kayaks.

● ● ● ● ● = 12 = twelve

1 2 3 4 5 6 7 8 9 10 11 **12** 13 14 15 16 17 18 19 20

People surf in the ocean. There are
13 surfers in the water.

= 13 = thirteen

1 2 3 4 5 6 7 8 9 10 11 12 **13** 14 15 16 17 18 19 20

Tennis balls are used to play tennis.
There are 14 tennis balls.

1 2 3 4 5 6 7 8 9 10 11 12 13 **14** 15 16 17 18 19 20

Bowling balls knock down pins.
There are 15 bowling balls.

= 15 = fifteen

1 2 3 4 5 6 7 8 9 10 11 12 13 14 **15** 16 17 18 19 20

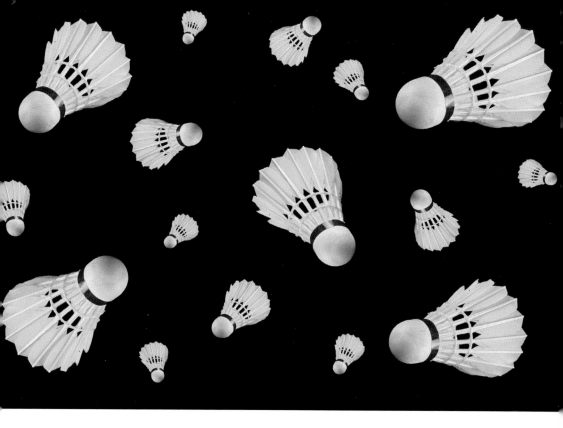

Birdies are hit over a net in **badminton**. There are 16 birdies.

= 16 = sixteen

1 2 3 4 5 6 7 8 9 10 11 12 13 14 15 **16** 17 18 19 20

People swim in the pool.
There are 17 kids in the pool.

= 17 = seventeen

1 2 3 4 5 6 7 8 9 10 11 12 13 14 15 16 **17** 18 19 20

Kaya climbs the wall. She holds the grips. There are 18 grips to her left.

= 18 = eighteen

1 2 3 4 5 6 7 8 9 10 11 12 13 14 15 16 17 **18** 19 20

The **golf** balls are on the grass.
There are 19 golf balls.

Archers shoot arrows. There are 20 arrows.

1 2 3 4 5 6 7 8 9 10 11 12 13 14 15 16 17 18 19 **20**

Glossary

archer – a person who uses a bow to shoot arrows.

badminton – a game in which the players use rackets to hit a shuttlecock or birdie over a high net.

birdie – an object hit by rackets in badminton. It is also called a shuttlecock.

croquet – a game in which players hit balls through hoops using mallets.

golf – a game in which players use clubs to try and hit a small white ball into a series of holes.

kayak – a small, narrow boat that you sit in and move with a paddle.

ski – to glide on narrow strips of wood, metal, or plastic attached to one's feet.

tennis – a game played by two or four players who use rackets to hit a ball over a net.